THE
PEOPLE

Native American
Thoughts and Feelings

DISCARD

BROWN SCHOOL LIBRARY

THE BOOK PUBLISHING COMPANY

SUMMERTOWN, TENNESSEE

815.008
HAM
9/99
#10.00

ACKNOWLEDGEMENTS

Editor: Roger Hammer
General Content: The People
Illustrations: Eleanor Dale Evans
Design: Eleanor Dale Evans and Ellen M. Isaacs

Book Publishing Company, Summertown, TN 38483

ISBN 0-913990-77-9

First Published by:
The Place In The Woods
Golden Valley, MN 55422

© Roger Hammer, 1990

PRINTED ON 100% POST CONSUMER
RECYCLED PAPER

The People : Native American thoughts and feelings / [editor, Roger Hammer].
       p. cm.
Originally published : Golden Valley, MN : Place in the Woods, 1975
ISBN 0-913990-77-9 (alk. paper) : $5.95
1. Indians of North America—Oratory. 2. Speeches, addresses, etc. American-Indian authors. 3. Indians of North America—Attitudes. 4. Indians of North America—History—Sources.
I. Hammer, Roger A., 1934-
E98.07P46 1991
815.008'0897—dc20   91-7567
                                       CIP

ALL RIGHTS RESERVED. No portion of this book may be resprduced by any means whatsoever, except for brief quotations in reviews, without written permission from the publisher.

INTRODUCTION

They have been called
"Indians"
and "Native Americans"
and "Native People."

They call themselves
simply
"The People."

Language of The People
is inseparable
from the culture —
they are one.

Words are chosen carefully,
to speak thoughts and feelings
as precisely
as a surgeon's knife.

Sometimes the words
cut through the inconsistencies
and lies of living
as surely as the scalpel.

Sometimes the words
are as gentle
as brittle leaves going to Mother Earth
from the weight of fresh snow flakes.

Some of the quotations
and writings in this work
are very short —
seeming to speak a single thought,
yet there is so much more.

Some of the passages
are long,
weaving a story as intricate and beautiful
as the blanket-maker's work.

Let the music in these pages
touch your eyes
and the thoughts and feelings
enter and move your spirit.

Know that they may have come
from deep, deep
in the center of the earth
where it all started.

Know that they have been carried
by the four winds
and scattered among The People
to be received by those who are ready.

You may find the thoughts and feelings
as fickle and fleeting
as the shapes of flames in a campfire
— and as hypnotizing.

You may discover them
as cold as ashes,
showing only powdery remains
of the rage and fire
that once was a living story.

The hope is
that you find them
— however you do it.

Find the feelings
and perhaps you'll discover
something in yourself.

R. HAMMER

Around the council fires tribal affairs were settled without benefit of the written word, and young men attended so that they could hear the speeches, observe their delivery, and consider the weight of reasoned argument. Speakers at tribal councils were men of eminence in war or council or both. They were also men of dignity and ability, well trained in the oral tradition. Their speeches, which would do credit to any Athenian orator, should dispel for all time the myth of the Indian as ignorant savage.

"What is life?
It is the flash of a firefly in the night.
It is the breath of a buffalo in the winter time.
It is the little shadow which runs across the grass
and loses itself in the Sunset."

CROWFOOT

"It was lonesome, the leaving. Husband dead, friends buried or held prisoners. I felt that I was leaving all that I had but I did not cry. You know how you feel when you lose kindred and friends through sickness — death. You do not care if you die. With us it was worse. Strong men, well women and little children killed and buried. They had not done wrong to be so killed. We had only asked to be left in our own homes, the homes of our ancestors. Our going was with heavy hearts, broken spirits. But we would be free...All lost, we walked silently on into the wintry night."

WETATONMI — Nez Perce 7

"In the life of the Indian there was only one inevitable duty — the duty of prayer — the daily recognition of the Unseen and Eternal. His daily devotions were more necessary to him than daily food. He wakes at daybreak, puts on his moccasins and steps down to the water's edge. Here he throws handfuls of clear, cold water into his face, or plunges in bodily. After the bath, he stands erect before the advancing dawn, facing the sun as it dances upon the horizon, and offers his unspoken orison. His mate may precede or follow him in his devotions, but never accompanies him. Each soul must meet the morning sun, the new sweet earth and the Great Silence alone!

"Whenever, in the course of the daily hunt the red hunter comes upon a scene that is strikingly beautiful or sublime — black thundercloud with the rainbow's glowing arch above the mountain, a white waterfall in the heart of a green gorge; a vast prairie tinged with the blood-red of sunset — the pauses for an instant in the attitude of worship. He sees no need for setting apart one day in seven as a holy day, since to him all days are God's."

OHIYESA

Tell General Howard I know his heart. What he told me before I have in my heart. I am tired of fighting. Our chiefs are killed. Looking Glass is dead. It is the young men who say yes or no. He who led the young men is dead. It is cold and we have no blankets. The little children are freezing to death. My people, some of them have run away to the hills and have no blankets, no food; no one knows where they are — perhaps freezing to death. I want to have time to look for my children and see how many I can find. Maybe I shall find them among the dead. Hear me my chiefs. I am tired; my heart is sick and sad. From where the sun now stands, I will fight no more forever.

CHIEF JOSEPH — Nez Perce

*"I had learned many English words
and could recite part of
the Ten Commandments.
I knew how to sleep on a bed, pray to Jesus,
comb my hair,
eat with a knife and fork,
and use a toilet...
I had also learned that a person
thinks with his head instead of his heart."*

SUN CHIEF — Hopi

"Behold, my brothers, the spring has come; the earth has received the embraces of the sun and we shall soon see the results of that love!

"Every seed is awakened and so has all animal life. It is through this mysterious power that we too have our being and we therefore yield to our neighbors, even our animal neighbors, the same right as ourselves, to inhabit this land.

"Yet, hear me, people, we have now to deal with another race — small and feeble when our fathers first met them but now great and overbearing. Strangely enough they have a mind to till the soil and the love of possession is a disease with them. These people have made many rules that the rich may break but the poor may not. They take tithes from the poor and weak to support the rich who rule. They claim this mother of ours, the earth, for their own and fence their neighbors away; they deface her with their buildings and refuse. That nation is like a spring freshet that overruns its banks and destroys all who are in its path.

"We cannot dwell side by side. Only seven years ago we made a treaty by which we were assured that the buffalo country should be left to us forever. Now they threaten to take that away from us. My brothers, shall we submit or shall we say to them: 'First kill me before you take possession of my Fatherland...'"

TATANKA YOTANKA or SITTING BULL — Hunkpapa Teton-Sioux

"I have seen two generations of my people die. Not a man of the two generations is alive now but myself. I know the difference between peace and war better than any man in my country. I am now grown old, and must die soon; my authority must descend to my brothers, Opitchapan, Opechancanough and Catatough — then to my two sisters, and then to my two daughters. I wish them to know as much as I do, and that your love to them may be like mine to you. Why will you destroy us who supply you with food? What can you get by war? We can hide our provisions and run into the woods; then you will starve for wronging your friends. Why are you jealous of us? We are unarmed, and willing to give you what you ask, if you come in a friendly manner, and not with swords and guns, as if to make war upon an enemy.

"I am not so simple as not to know that it is much better to each good meat, sleep comfortably, live quietly with my wives and children, laugh and be merry with the English, and trade for their copper and hatchets, than to run away from them, and to lie cold in the woods, feed on acorns, roots and such trash, and be so hunted that I can neither eat or sleep. In these wars, my men must sit up watching, and if a twig break, they all cry out, 'Here comes Captain Smith!' So I must end my miserable life. Take away your guns and swords, the cause of all our jealousy, or you may all die in the same manner."

WAHUNSONACOCK – Powhatan

15

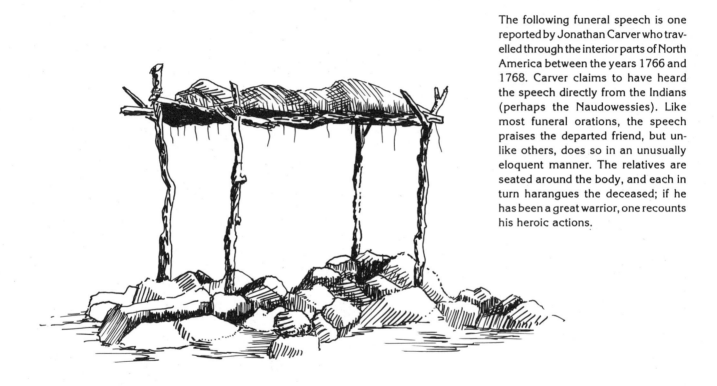

The following funeral speech is one reported by Jonathan Carver who travelled through the interior parts of North America between the years 1766 and 1768. Carver claims to have heard the speech directly from the Indians (perhaps the Naudowessies). Like most funeral orations, the speech praises the departed friend, but unlike others, does so in an unusually eloquent manner. The relatives are seated around the body, and each in turn harangues the deceased; if he has been a great warrior, one recounts his heroic actions.

"You still sit among us, brother, your person retains its usual resemblance and continues similar to ours, without any visible deficiency except that it has lost the power of action. But wither is that breath flown, which a few hours ago sent up breath to the Great Spirit? Why are those lips silent, that lately delivered to us expressive and pleasing language? Why are those feet motionless that a short time ago were fleeter than the deer on yonder mountains? Why useless hang those arms that could climb the tallest tree, or draw the toughest bow? Alas! Every part of that frame which we lately beheld with admiration and wonder, is now become as inanimate as it was three hundred winters ago. We will not, however, bemoan thee as if thou wast forever lost to us, or that thy name would be buried in oblivion; thy soul yet lives in the great country of Spirits, with those of thy nation that are gone before thee; and though we are left behind to perpetuate thy fame, we shall one day join thee. Actuated by the respect we bore thee whilst living, we now come to tender to thee the last act of kindness it is in our power to bestow: that thy body might not lie neglected on the plain, and become a prey to the beasts of the field, or the fowls of the air, we will take care to lay it with those of thy predecessors who are gone before thee; hoping at the same time, that thy spirit will feed with their spirits, and be ready to receive ours, when we also shall arrive at the great Country of Souls."

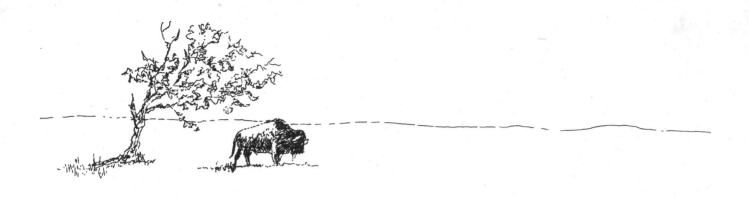

"Our land is more valuable than your money. It will last forever. It will not even perish by the flames of fire. As long as the sun shines and the waters flow, this land will be here to give life to men and animals; therefore we cannot sell this land. It was put here for us by the Great Spirit and we cannot sell it because it does not belong to us. You can count your money and burn it within the nod of a buffalo's head, but only the Great Spirit can count the grains of sand and the blades of grass of these plains. As a present to you, we will give you anything we have that you can take with you; but the land, never."

Blackfeet Chief

BROWN SCHOOL LIBRARY

"The earth was created by the assistance of the sun, and it should be left as it was...The country was made without lines of demarcation, and it is no man's business to divide it...I see the whites all over the country gaining wealth, and see their desire to give us lands which are worthless...The earth and myself are of one mind. The measure of the land and the measure of our bodies are the same. Say to us if you can say it, that you were sent by the Creative Power to talk to us. Perhaps you think the Creator sent you here to dispose of us as you see fit. If I thought you were sent by the Creator I might be induced to think you had a right to dispose of me. Do not misunderstand me, but understand me fully with reference to my affection for the land. I never said the land was mine to do with as I chose. The one who has the right to dispose of it is the one who created it. I claim a right to live on my land, and accord you the privilege to live on yours."

CHIEF JOSEPH — Nez Perce

"We were on pretty good terms with the Great Spirit, creator and ruler of all. You whites assumed we were savages. You didn't understand our prayers. You didn't try to understand. When we sang our praises to the sun or moon or wind, you said we were worshipping idols. Without understanding, you condemned us as lost souls just because our form of worship was different from yours.

"We saw the Great Spirit's work in almost everything: sun, moon, trees, wind, and mountains. Sometimes we approached him through these things. Was that so bad?

"I think we have a true belief in the supreme being, a stronger faith than that of most whites who have called us pagans...Indians living close to nature and nature's ruler are not living in darkness.

"Did you know that trees talk? Well they do. They talk to each other, and they'll talk to you if you listen. Trouble is, white people don't listen. They never learned to listen to the Indians so I don't suppose they'll listen to other voices in nature. But I have learned a lot from trees: sometimes about the weather, sometimes about animals, sometimes about the Great Spirit."

TATANGA MANI or Walking Buffalo — Stoney Nation

"Brothers! I have listened to many talks from our great father. When he first came over the wide waters, he was but a little man...very little. His legs were cramped by sitting long in his big boat, and he begged for a little land to light his fire on...But when the little man had warmed himself before the Indians' fire and filled himself with their hominy, he became very large. With a step he bestrode the mountains, and his feet covered the plains and the valleys. His hand grasped the eastern and the western sea, and his head rested on the moon. Then he became our Great Father. He loved his red children, and he said, 'Get a little further, lest I tread on thee...'

"Brothers I have listened to a great many talks from our great father. But they always began and ended in this — 'Get a little further; you are too near me.'"

SPECKLED SNAKE — Creek Nation

"Thou reproachest us very inappropriately, that our country is a little hell on earth in contrast with France, which thou comparest to a terrestrial paradise, inasmuch as it yields thee, so thou sayest, every kind of provision in abundance. Thou sayest of us also that we are the most miserable and unhappy of all men, living without religion, without manners, without honor, without social order, and in a word, without any rules, like the beasts in our woods and forests, lacking bread, wine, and a thousand other comforts, which thou hast in superfluity in Europe. Well, my brother, if thou doest not yet know the real feelings which our Indians have towards thy Country and towards all thy nation, it is proper that I inform thee at once.

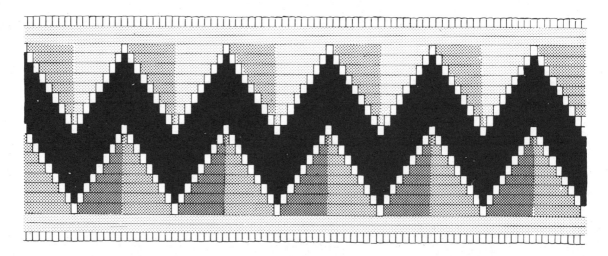

I beg thee now to believe that, all miserable as we seem in thy eyes, we consider ourselves nevertheless much happier than thou, in this that we are very content with the little that we have...Thou deceivest thyselves greatly if thou thinkest to persuade us that thy country is better than ours. For if France, as thou sayest, is a little terrestrial paradise, art thou sensible to leave it? And why abandon wives, children, relatives, and friends? Why risk thy life and thy property every year? And why venture thyself with such risk in any season whatsoever, to the storms and tempests of the sea in order to come to a strange and barbarous country which thou considerest the poorest and least fortunate of the world. Besides, since we are wholly convinced of the

contrary, we scarcely take the trouble to go to France because we fear with good reason, lest we find little satisfaction there, seeing in our own experience that those who are natives thereof leave it every year in order to enrich themselves on our shores. We believe, further, that you are also incomparably poorer than we, and that you are only simple journeymen, valets, servants, and slaves, all masters and Grand Captains though you may appear, seeing that you glory in our old rags, and in our miserable suits of beaver which can no longer be of use to us, and that you find among us in the fishery for cod which you make in these parts, the wherewithal to comfort your misery and poverty which oppress you. As to us, we find all our riches and all our conveniences

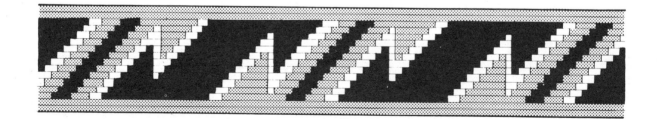

among ourselves, without trouble, without exposing our lives to the dangers in which you find yourselves constantly through your long voyages. And whilst feeling compassion for you in the sweetness of our repose, we wonder at the anxieties and cares which you give yourselves, night and day, in order to load your ships. We see also that all your people live, as a rule, only upon cod which you catch among us. It is everlastingly nothing but cod; cod in the morning, cod at midday, cod at evening, and always cod, until things come to pass that if you wish some good morsels at our expense; and you are obliged to have recourse to the Indians, whom you despise so much, and to beg them to go a-hunting that you may be regaled. Now tell me this one little thing, if you

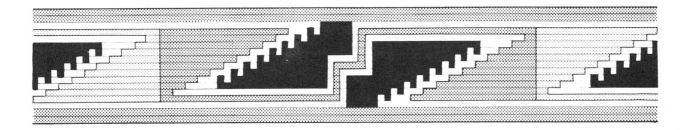

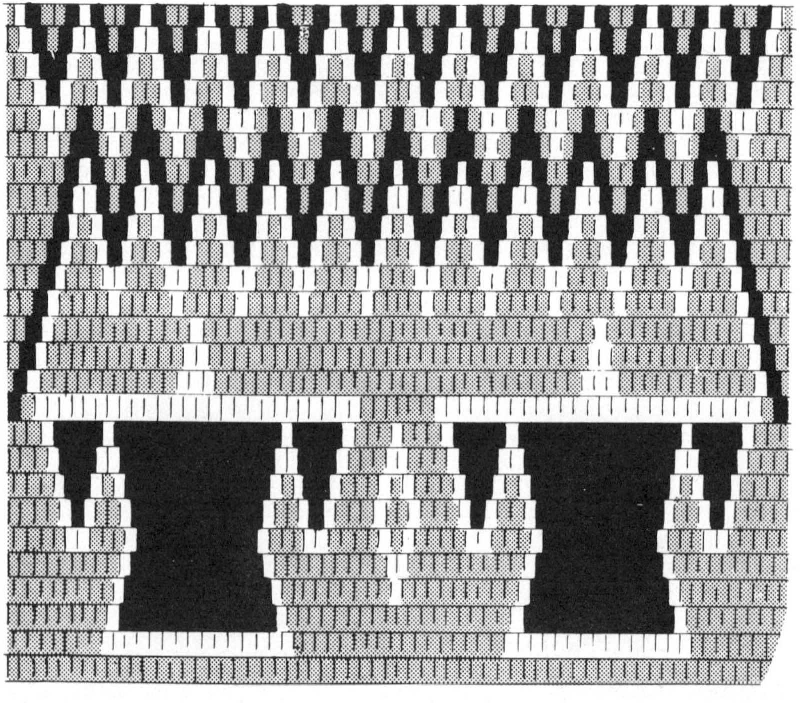

hast any sense, which of these two is the wisest and happiest: he who labors with ceasing and only obtains...with great trouble, enough to live on, or he who rests in comfort and finds all that he needs in the pleasure of hunting and fishing.

It is true that we have always had the use of bread and of wine which your France produces; but, in fact, before the arrival of the French in these parts, did not the Gaspesians live much longer than now? And if we have not any longer among us any of those old men of a hundred and thirty to forty years, it is only because we are gradually adopting your manner of living, for experience is making it very plain that those of us live longest who, despising your bread, your wine, and your brandy, are content with their natural food of beaver, of moose, of waterfowl, and fish, in accord with the custom of our ancestors and of all the Gaspesian nation. Learn now, my brother once for all, because I must open to thee my heart: there is no Indian who does not consider himself infinitely more happy and more powerful than the French."

MICMAC — Indian Chief

"Where today is the Pequot?

Where are the Narragansetts, the Mohawks,

the Pokanoket,

and many other once powerful tribes

of our people?

They have vanished before the avarice and

the oppression of the White Man,

as snow before a summer sun."

TECUMSEH – Shawnee Chief

"I can remember that winter of the hundred slain (1866) as a man may remember some bad dream he dreamed when he was little, but I can not tell just how much I heard when I was bigger and how much I understood when I was little. It is like some fearful thing in a fog, for it was a time when everything seemed troubled and afraid.

"I had never seen a Wasichu (white man) then, and did not know what one looked like; but everyone was saying that the Wasichus were coming and that they were going to take our country and rub us all out and that we should all have to die fighting.

"Once we were happy in our country and we were seldom hungry, for then the two-leggeds and the four-leggeds lived together like relatives, and there was plenty for them and us. But the Wasichus came, and they have made little islands for us and other little islands for the four-leggeds, and always these islands are becoming smaller, for around them surges the gnawing flood of the Wasichu; and it is dirty with lies and greed.

"I was ten years old that winter, and the was the first time I ever saw a Wasichu. At first I thought they all looked sick, and I was afraid they might just begin to fight us at any time, but I got used to them.

"I can remember when the bison were so many that they could not be counted, but more and more Wasichus came to kill them until there were only heaps of bones scattered where they used to be. The Wasichus did not kill them to eat; they killed them for the metal that makes them crazy, and they took only the hides to sell. Sometimes they did not even take the hides, only the tongues; they just killed and killed because they liked to do that. When we hunted bison, we killed only what we needed."

HEHAKA SAPA or BLACK ELK — Great Sioux Chief

"That land of Ganono-o, or 'Empire State' as you love to call it, was once laced by our trails from Albany to Buffalo — trails that we had trod for centuries — trails worn so deep by the feet of the Iroquois that they became your own roads of travel as your possessions gradually eat into those of my people. Your roads still traverse those same lines of communication and bind one part of the Long House to another. The land of Ganono-o, the Empire State, then is our monument! We shall not long occupy much room in living; the single tree of thousands which sheltered our forefathers — one old elm under which the representatives of the tribes were wont to meet — will cover us all; but we would have our bodies twined in death among its roots, on the very soil on whence it grew! Perhaps it will last no longer being fertilized by their decay...

"In your last war with England, your red brother — your elder brother — still came up to help you as of old on the Canada frontier! Have we, the first holders of this prosperous region, no longer a share in your history? Glad were your fathers to sit upon the threshold of the Long House, rich did they hold themselves in getting the mere sweeping from its door.

"Had our forefathers spurned you from it when the French were thundering at the opposite end to get a passage through and drive you into the sea? Whatever has been the fate of other Indians, the Iroquois might have been a nation; and I instead of pleading for the privilege of living within your borders — I — I — might have had a country!"

WA-O-WO-WA-NO-ONK (Dr. Peter Wilson) — Cayuga chief

"The tipi is much better to live in; always clean, warm in winter, cool in summer; easy to move. The white man builds big house, cost much money, like big cage, shut out sun, can never move; always sick. Indians and animals know better how to live than white man; nobody can be in good health if he does not have all the time fresh air, sunshine and good water. If the Great Spirit wanted men to stay in one place he would make the world stand still; but He made it to always change, so birds and animals can move and always have green grass and ripe berries, sunlight to work and play, and night to sleep; always changing; everything for good; nothing for nothing. The white man does not obey the Great Spirit; that is why the Indians never agree with him."

CHIEF FLYING HAWK — Oglala Sioux

"My young men shall never work.
men who work cannot dream;
and wisdom comes to us in dreams.
You ask me to plow the ground.
Shall I take a knife
and tear my mother's breast?
Then when I die she will not
take me to her bosom to rest.
You ask me to dig for stone.
Shall I dig under her skin for her bones?
Then when I die I cannot
enter her body to be born again.
You ask me to cut grass
and make hay and sell it
and be rich like white men.
But how dare I cut off
my mother's hair?"

SMOHALLA SOKULK — Nez Perce

"My people are few. They resemble the scattering trees of a storm-swept plain...There was time when our people covered the land as the waves of a wind-ruffled sea cover its shell-paved floor, but that time long since passed away with the greatness of tribes that are now but a mournful memory...

"To us the ashes of our ancestors are sacred and the resting place is hallowed ground. You wander far from the graves of your ancestors and seemingly without regret. Your religion was written on tables of stone by the iron finger of your God so that you could not forget. The Red Man could never comprehend nor remember it. Our religion is the traditions of our ancestors — the dreams of our old men, given them in the solemn hours of night by the Great Spirit; and the visions of our sachems, and is written in the hearts of our people.

"Your dead cease to love you and the land of their nativity as soon as they pass the portals of the tomb and wander away beyond the stars. They are soon forgotten and never return. Our dead never forget the beautiful world that gave them being.

"When the last Red Man shall have perished, and the memory of my tribe shall have become a myth among the white man, these shores will swarm with the invisible dead of my tribe, and when your childrens' children think themselves alone in the field, the store, the shop, or in the silence of the pathless woods, they will not be alone...At night when the streets of your cities and villages are silent and you think them deserted, they will throng with the returning hosts that once filled them and still love this beautiful land. The White Man will never be alone.

"Let him be just and deal kindly with my people, for the dead are not powerless. Dead — I say? There is no death. Only a change of worlds."

CHIEF SEATTLE — Dwamish Tribe 43

"We always had plenty; our children never cried from hunger, neither were our people in want... The rapids of Rock River furnished us with an abundance of excellent fish, and the land being very fertile, never failed to produce good crops of corn, beans, pumpkins, and squashes...Here our village stood for more than a hundred years, during all of which time we were the undisputed possessors of the Mississippi Valley...Our village was healthy and there was no place in the country possessing such advantages, nor hunting grounds better than those we had in possession. If a prophet had come to our village in those days and told us that the things were to take place which have since come to pass, none of our people would have believed him."

MA-KA-TAI-ME-SHE-KIA-KIAK or BLACK HAWK —
Chief of the Sauk and Fox

On June 17, 1744, the commissioners from Maryland and Virginia negotiated a treaty with the Indians of the Six Nations at Lancaster, Pennsylvania. The Indians were invited to send boys to William and Mary College. The next day they declined the offer as follows.

"We know that you highly esteem the kind of learning taught in those Colleges, and that the Maintenance of our young Men, while with you, would be very expensive to you. We are convinced, that you mean to do us Good by your Proposal; and we thank you heartily. But you, who are wise must know that different Nations have different Conceptions of things and you will therefore not take it amiss, if our Ideas of this kind of Education happen not to be the same as yours. We have had some Experience of it. Several of our young People were formerly brought up at the Colleges of the Northern Provinces: they were instructed in all your Sciences; but, when they came back to us, they were bad Runners, ignorant of every means of living in the woods...neither fit for Hunters, Warriors, nor Counsellors, they were totally good for nothing.

"We are, however, not the less oblig'd by your kind Offer, tho' we decline accepting it; and, to show our grateful Sense of it, if the Gentlemen of Virginia will send us a Dozen of their Sons, we will take Care of their Education, instruct them in all we know, and make Men of them."

"The ground on which we stand is sacred ground. It is the dust and blood of our ancestors. On these plains the Great White Father at Washington sent his soldiers armed with long knives and rifles to slay the Indian. Many of them sleep on yonder hill where Pahaska — White Chief of the Long Hair (General Custer) — so bravely fought and fell. A few more passing suns will see us here no more, and our dust and bones will mingle with these same prairies.

I see as in a vision the dying spark of our council fires, the ashes cold and white. I see no longer the curling smoke rising from our lodge poles. I hear no longer the songs of the women as they prepare the meal. The antelope have gone; the buffalo wallows are empty. Only the wail of the coyote is heard. The white man's medicine is stronger than ours; his iron horse rushes over the buffalo trail. He talks to us through his 'whispering spirit' (the telephone). We are like birds with a broken wing. My heart is cold within me. My eyes are growing dim — I am old..."

"My brothers, the Indians must always be remembered in this land. Out of our languages we have given names to many beautiful things which will always speak of us. Minnehaha will laugh of us, Seneca will shine in our image, Mississippi will murmur our woes. The broad Iowa and the rolling Dakota and fertile Michigan will whisper our names to the sun that kisses them. The roaring Niagara, the sighing Illinois, the singing Delaware, will chant unceasingly our Dta-wa-e (Death Song). Can it be that your and your children will hear that eternal song without a stricken heart? We have been guilty of only one sin-we have had possessions that the white man coveted. We moved away toward the setting sun; we gave up our homes to the white man.

"My brethren, among the legends of my people it is told how a chief, leading the remnant of his people, crossed a great river, and striking his tipi-stake upon the ground, exclaimed 'A-la-ba-ma!' This in our language means 'Here we may rest!' But he saw not the future. The white man came: he and his people could not rest there; they were driven out, and in a dark swamp they were thrust down into the slime and killed. The word he so sadly spoke has given a name to one of the white man's states. There is no spot under those stars that now smile upon us, where the Indian can plant his foot and sigh 'Alabama.' It may be that Wakanda will grant us such a place. But it seems that it will be only at His side."

KHE-THA-A-HI or EAGLE WING 49

"Nay, you are miserable enough already, and indeed I can't see how you can be more such. What sort of Men must the EUROPEANS be? What Species of Creatures do they retain to? The EUROPEANS, who must be forc'd to do Good, and have no other Prompter for the avoiding of Evil than the fear of Punishment. If I ask'd thee, what a Man is, thou wouldst answer me, He's a FRENCHMAN, and yet I'll prove that your MAN is rather a BEAVER. For MAN is not entitled to that character upon the force of his walking upright upon two Legs, or of Reading and Writing, and showing a Thousand other Instances of his Industry...

"Who gave you all the Countries that you now inhabit, by what right do you possess them? They always belonged to the ALGONKINS before. In earnest, my dear Brother, I'm sorry for thee from the bottom of my soul. Take my advice, and turn HURON; for I see plainly a vast difference between thy condition and mine. I am Master of my Condition and mine. I am Master of my own Body, I have the absolute disposal of my self, I do what I please, I am the first and the last of my Nation, I fear no Man, and I depend only upon the Great Spirit. Whereas, thy Body, as well as thy Soul, are doomed to a dependence upon thy great captain, thy Vice-Roy disposes of thee, thou hast not the liberty of doing what thou hast a mind to; thou art afraid of Robbers, false Witnesses, Assassins, etc., and thou dependest upon an infinity of Persons whose Places have raised them above thee. Is is true or not?"

KONDIARONK — Huron Chief

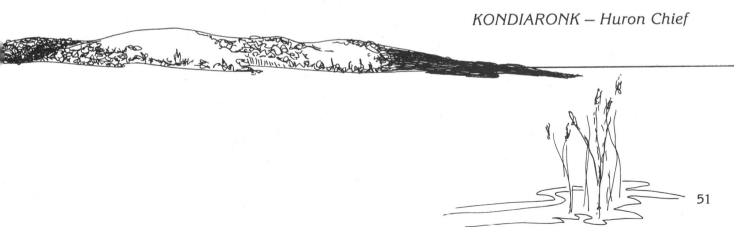

51

"The White Man does not understand the Indian for the reason that he does not America. He is too far removed from its formative processes. The root of the tree of his life have not yet grasped the rock and soil. The white man is still troubled with primitive fears; he still has in his consciousness the perils of this frontier continent, some of its vastnesses not yet having yielded to his questing footsteps and inquiring eyes. He shudders still with the memory of the loss of his forefathers upon its scorching deserts and forbidding mountain-tops. The man from Europe is still a foreigner and an alien. And he still hates the man who questioned his path across the continent. But in the Indian the spirit of the land is still vested; it will be until other men are able to divine and meet its rhythm. Men must be born and reborn to belong. Their bodies must be formed of the dust of their forefather's bones."

CHIEF LUTHER STANDING BEAR

"We did not ask you white men to come here. The Great Spirit gave us this country as a home. You had yours. We did not interfere with you. The Great Spirit gave us plenty of land to live on, and buffalo, deer, antelope and other game. But you have come here; you are taking my land from me; you are killing off our game, so it is hard for us to live. Now, you tell us to work for a living, but the Great Spirit did not make us to work, but to live by hunting. You white men can work if you want to. We do not interfere with you, and again you say, why do you not become civilized? We do not want your civilization! We would live as our fathers did, and their fathers before them."

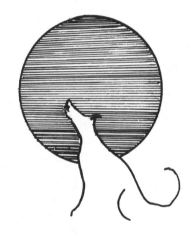

CRAZY HORSE —Oglala Sioux

"They do us no good. If they are not useful to the white people and do them no good, why do they send them among the Indians? If they are useful to the white people and do them good, why do they not keep them at home? They (the white men) are surely bad enough to need the labor of everyone who can make them better. These men (the missionaries) know we do not understand their religion. We cannot read their book — they tell us different stories about what it contains, and we believe they make the book talk to suit themselves.

If we had no money, no land and no country to be cheated out of these black coats would not trouble themselves about our good hereafter.

The Great Spirit will not punish us for what we do not know. He will do justice to his red children. These black coats talk to the Great Spirit, and ask for light that we may see as they do, when they are blind themselves and quarrel about the light that guides them. These things we do not understand, and the light which they give us makes the straight and plain path trod by our fathers, dark and dreary. The black coats tell us to work and raise corn; they do nothing themselves and would starve to death if someone did not feed them. All they do is to pray to the Great Spirit;

but that will not make corn and potatoes grow; if it will why do they beg from us and from the white people?

The red men knew nothing of trouble until it came from the white men; as soon as they crossed the great waters they wanted our country, and in return have always been ready to teach us to quarrel about their religion. Red Jacket can never be the friend of such men. If they (the Indians) were raised among white people, and learned to work and read as they do, it would only make their situation worse...We are few and weak, but may for a long time be happy if we hold fast to our country, and the religion of our fathers."

RED JACKET

"Oh, yes, I went to the white man's schools.
I learned to read from school books, newspapers,
and the Bible. But in time I found that these were not enough.
Civilized people depend too much on man-made printed pages.
I turn to the Great Spirit's book
which is the whole of his creation. You can read a
big part of that book if you study nature.
You know, if you take all your books, lay them out under the sun,
and let the snow and rain and insects work on them for a while,
there will be nothing left. But the Great Spirit has provided
you and me with an opportunity
for study in nature's university, the forests, the rivers, the
mountains, and the animals which include us."

TATANGA MANI — Stoney Nation

"What treaty that the whites have kept has the red man broken? Not one. What treaty that the white man ever made with us have they kept? Not one. When I was a boy the Sioux owned the world; the sun rose and set on their land; they sent ten thousand men to battle. Where are the warriors today? Who slew them? Where are our lands? Who owns them? What white man can say I ever stole his land or a penny of his money? Yet, they say I am a thief. What white woman, however lonely, was ever captive or insulted by me? Yet they say I am a bad Indian. What white man has ever seen me drunk? Who has ever come to me hungry and unfed? Who has ever seen me beat my wives or abuse my children? What law have I broken? Is it wrong for me to love my own? Is it wicked for me because my skin is red? Because I am a Sioux; because I was born where my father lived; because I would die for my people and my country?"

SITTING BULL

POSTSCRIPT

Roger Hammer and I came together first in 1970 at the University of Minnesota. I was teaching Ojibwe language, culture and philosophy in the department of American Indian Studies. He was seeking a more meaningful life.
I have since determined him to be one of the most beautiful, compassionate people I know. This is profound because he is European-American and I am Anishinabe of the Objibwe tongue and Wazhushk Clan.
He speaks 'English' and yet, even though he started his thinking from a 'white man's' frame of thought, he has learned to be more considerate of all things.
I am a native Ojibwe speaker and learned as a child a much different world view. We are a part of the whole universe-world — animals, people, etc. — and have respect for all.
Roger is thoughtful (he won't build a bonfire on the bare earth), kind (he has done many projects of help others) and generous (he published 'The People' as a non-profit effort).
I have gotten to know this friend well over the years.

'The People' is the result of evolution in Roger's mind. He has found these new truths to be important and overpowering to him. As he internalized the new thoughts and spoke out, I thought 'He's really not very different from us at all.'

He became increasingly anxious to share these newly found joys with both the Anishinabe and other people.

Being a writer with a background in newspaper, magazine and wire service journalism, he sought a way to communicate with his talent what he was learning about the People. He finally told me, 'Why should I try and write beautiful things about the People when they are so eloquent themselves?'

With that, he decided to compile 'The People' using the original People's words as quoted.

I feel this is a fair, kind, thoughtful and wise endeavor. It should be enjoyed by as many people as possible.

Me Gwetch (I give thanks)

Humbly,

Mizinokamigok

These fine Native American books are available at your local bookstore or from:

The Book Publishing Company
PO Box 99
Summertown, TN 38483

1-800-695-2241

Please include $2. per book for postage and handling.

BROWN SCHOOL
LIBRARY

Basic Call to Consciousness	$7.95
Blackfoot Craftworker's Book	$11.95
Children of the Circle	$9.95
Dream Feather	$11.95
Good Medicine Collection:	
Life in Harmony with Nature	$9.95
How Can One Sell the Air? Chief Seattle's Vision	
(NEW edition)	$6.95
Indian Tribes of the Northern Rockies	$9.95
Legends Told by the Old People	$5.95
A Natural Education	$5.95
The People: Native American	
Thoughts and Feelings	$5.95
The Powwow Calendar (Annual Guide	
to Native American Cultural Events)	$6.95
Sacred Song of the Hermit Thrush	$5.95
Song of the Seven Herbs	$10.95
Song of the Wild Violets	$5.95
Spirit of the White Bison	$5.95
Teachings of Nature	$8.95
Traditional Dress	$5.95